VOCAL SELECTIONS

BE MORE CHILL
MUSIC AND LYRICS BY JOE ICONIS

Three more songs are available at **www.sheetmusicdirect.us**

The Pitiful Children
The Smartphone Hour (Rich Set a Fire)
Upgrade

ISBN 978-1-5400-0712-4

7777 W. BLUEMOUND RD. P.O. BOX 13819 MILWAUKEE, WI 53213

In Australia Contact:
Hal Leonard Australia Pty. Ltd.
4 Lentara Court
Cheltenham, Victoria, 3192 Australia
Email: ausadmin@halleonard.com.au

Visit Hal Leonard Online at
www.halleonard.com

JEREMY'S THEME

Music by
JOE ICONIS

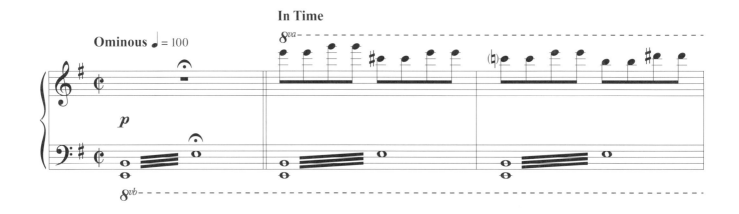

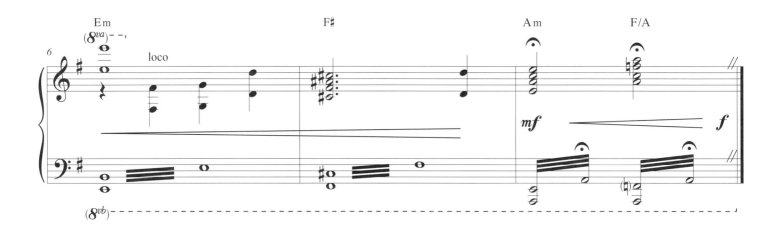

MORE THAN SURVIVE

Words and Music by
JOE ICONIS

rules and I use them as my tools to stay_____ a - live I don't wan-na be

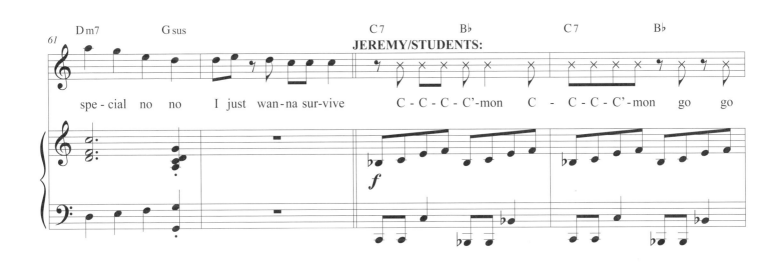

JEREMY/STUDENTS:

spe - cial no no I just wan-na sur-vive C - C - C - C'-mon C - C - C - C'-mon go go

C - C - C - C'-mon C - C - C - C'-mon go go

8

JEREMY: *You're listening to
Bob Marley again, aren't you?*

the roll is ne - gi - ma - ki and I'm feel - in' kind - a cock - y 'cuz the

girl at sev' - e - lev' gave me a gen - er - ous pour __ I'm

lis - ten - ing to Mar - ley and the groove is hel - la gnar - ly and we're al - most at the end of the song

yeah that was the end now tell me friend how was

I LOVE PLAY REHEARSAL

Words and Music by
JOE ICONIS

CHRISTINE: Where
was I? Oh, right!

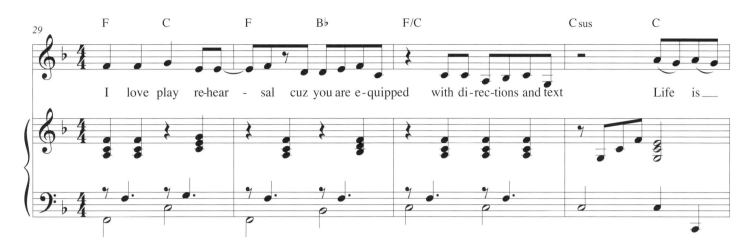

I love play re-hear - sal cuz you are e - quipped with di - rec-tions and text Life is___

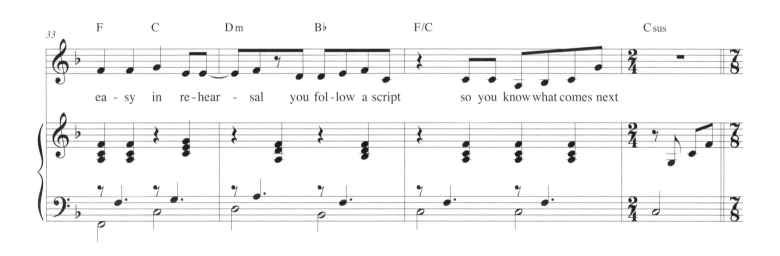

ea - sy in re - hear - sal you fol - low a script so you know what comes next

Colla Voce - SUPER FAST

An - y - hoo the point that I'm get - ting to is some - times life can't

A Tempo

work out in ___ the way it works out in ___ the play like the on - ly time ___ I

get to be ___ the cen - ter of ___ at - ten - tion is when I'm Ju - li -

CHRISTINE: ...that was really one of my best roles, did you see that? I was incredibly commanding, I think. It made me feel like there just aren't strong roles for women in theater these days, particularly high school theater, do you find that? Because I totally find that— [SHE SINGS]

et or Blanche Du - Bois, and can ___ I men - tion and

no mat - ter how hard I try it's im -

CHRISTINE: *There's also a part of me that wants to do this. [CRAZY GOBLIN NOISE] So I did it!*

THE SQUIP SONG

Words and Music by
JOE ICONIS

Rock Out - Faster!

TWO-PLAYER GAME

Words and Music by
JOE ICONIS

Agh! Oh! Zom-bie!

Blood! Claws! Pause...

Colla Voce

JEREMY: You know that you are my fav - 'rite per - son. That

does - n't mean I can't still dream. MICHAEL: Is it real - ly true? I'm your

BE MORE CHILL/
DO YOU WANNA RIDE?

Words and Music by
JOE ICONIS

SQUIP: Brooke is going to offer you a ride. It is imperative you accept.
BROOKE: So...[SHE SINGS]

DO YOU WANNA RIDE?

Half-Time Feel

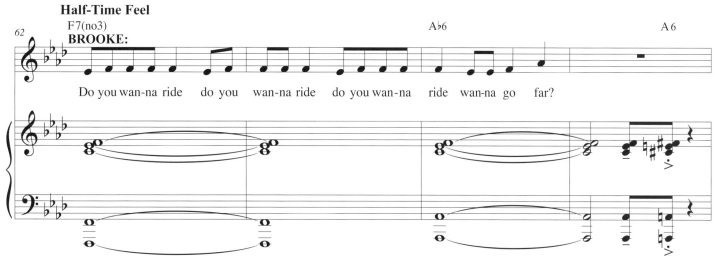

Do you wan-na ride   do you   wan-na ride   do you wan-na   ride wan-na go   far?

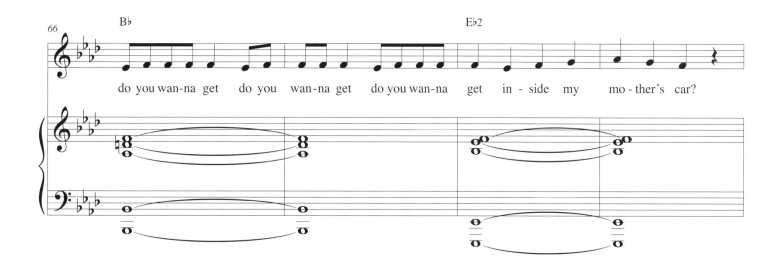

do you wan-na get   do you   wan-na get   do you wan-na   get in - side my   mo-ther's car?

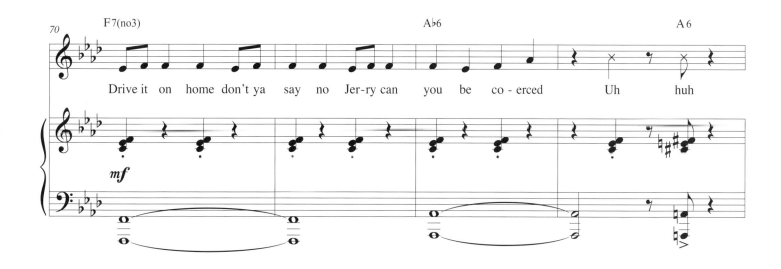

Drive it on   home don't ya   say no Jer-ry can   you be co-erced   Uh   huh

50

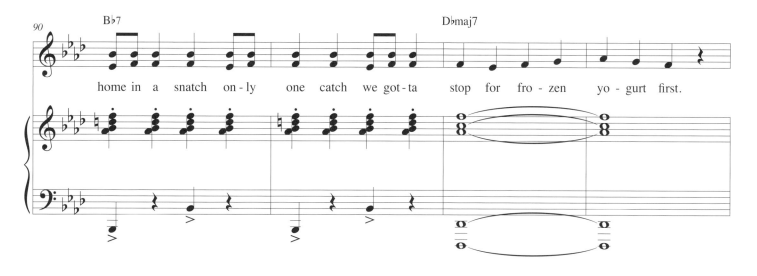

home in a snatch on-ly one catch we got-ta stop for fro-zen yo-gurt first.

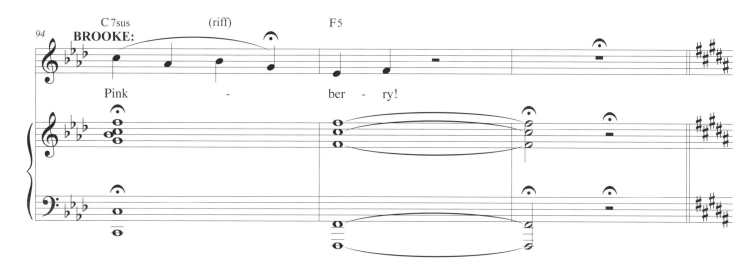

BROOKE:

Pink - ber - ry!

BE MORE CHILL PART 2

Colla Voce

SQUIP:

oh _____ ev-ery-thing _ a-bout you is so ter-rib-le

JEREMY:

ev - ery-thing _ a-bout me is just ter-rib-le

52

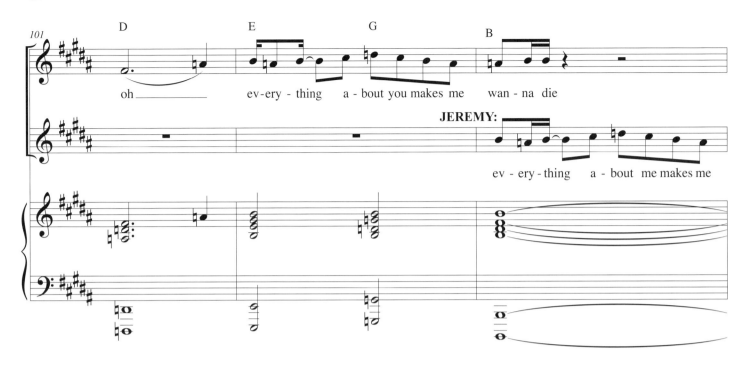

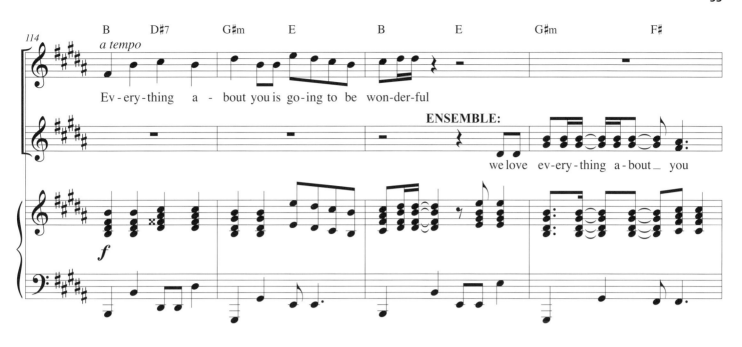

A GUY THAT I'D KINDA BE INTO

Words and Music by
JOE ICONIS

Say there's this per-son you pass___ in the hall___ ev-ry day. You've

known him since sev-enth grade. You're used to think-ing a-bout___ him in a cer - tain

way from the per - son - a that he dis-played. Then some-thing chang-

HALLOWEEN

Words and Music by
JOE ICONIS

Original Feel

It's Hal - low-een   It's Hal - low-een

Crank the bass It's Hal - low-een   break a vase It's Hal - low-een

Jel - lo shots It's Hal - low - een   liv - er spots from Hal - low-een

mf

MICHAEL IN THE BATHROOM

Words and Music by
JOE ICONIS

Tempo I

THE PANTS SONG

Words and Music by
JOE ICONIS

VOICES IN MY HEAD

Words and Music by
JOE ICONIS

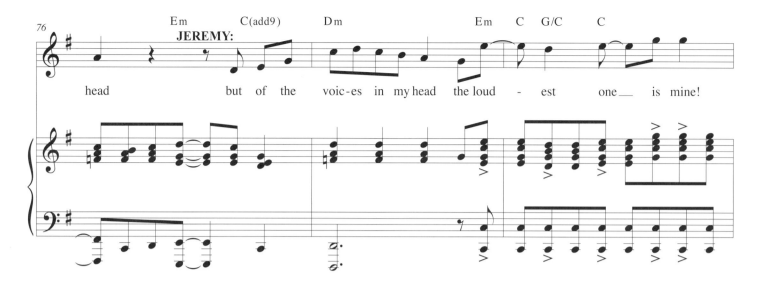

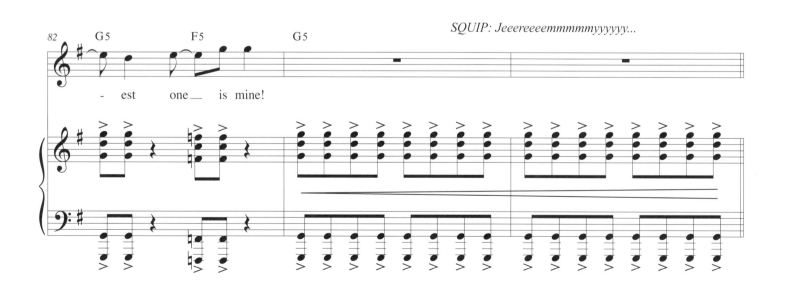

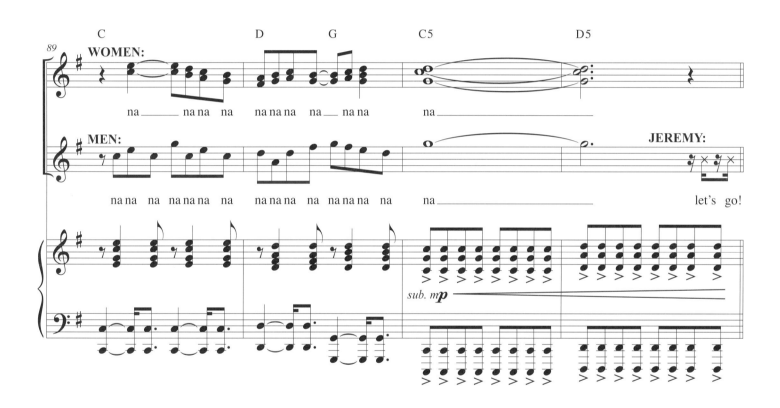

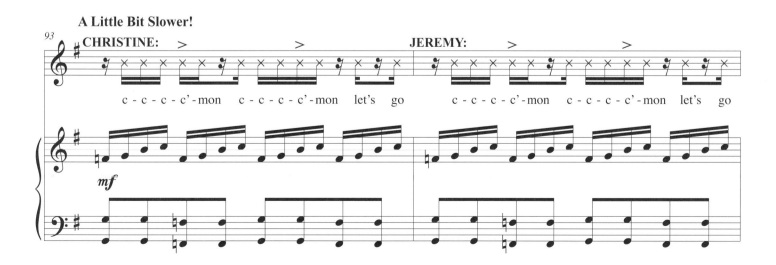

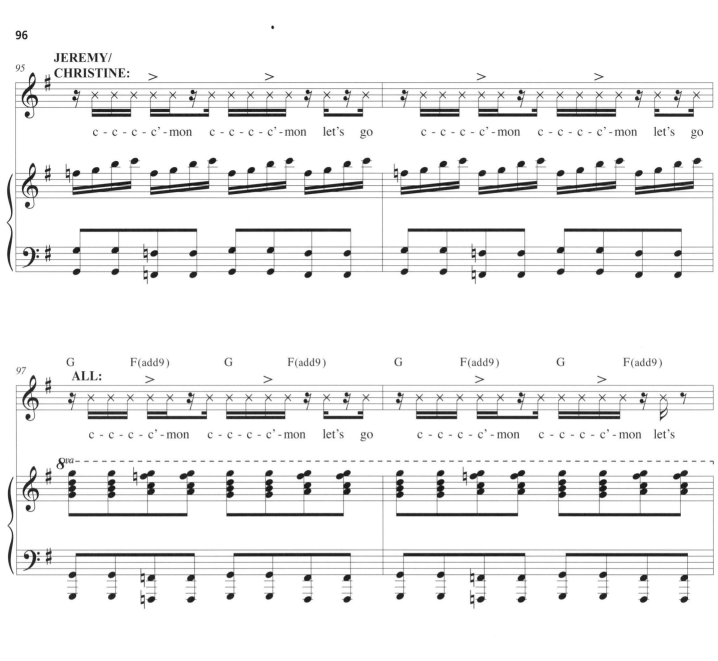

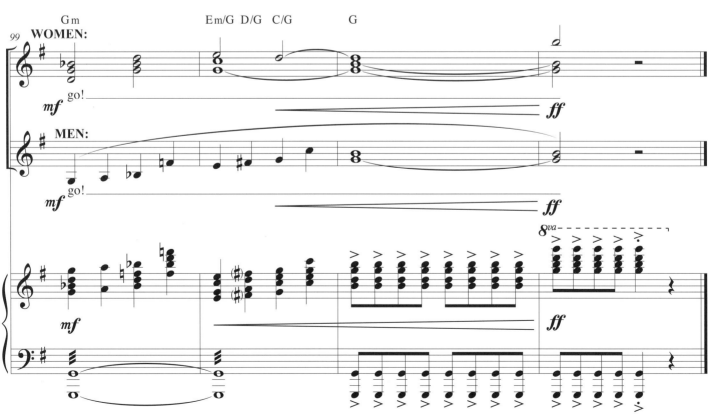